Introduction

MORE THAN CONQUERORS!

The world has been altered forever. The effects of the Corona Virus are already making drastic changes in our attitudes and outlooks. God is not surprised, and He will turn it all out for good for this that love Him and are called according to His purpose, so we need not fear. He said that His people perish for a lack of knowledge. He also said without a vision we will perish. That is why I am putting years of notes and adult Sunday School lessons into books to give you some things to chew on while you transition into the new world that is about to emerge. There are varied subjects. I am sure you will find one that interests you. My goal is to give you a renewed hunger for the Word of God without which we literally cannot survive. May Jesus rule and reign in your heart!

Judy Parrott

Titles

3 What Is It All About?
8 Yes, There Is A War Going On
13 Why pray? How pray? When pray?
18 Why Miracles?
28 Find Those That Manifest Gifts
30 Why Hide The Word?
36 My People Perish For Lack Of Knowledge
41 What is Repentance?
42 We Are All Worshippers
45 Jesus Calling
46 What is a Soultie?
50 Walking With Jesus
58 Greater Than Love?
63 Things To Chew On
66 The Salesman
68 The No Worry Zone
70 The Secret Of Power With God
71 The Man with no Name
73 The Light Overcomes The Darkness
75 The Last Days
76 Superman, An Allegory Of Jesus?
78 The Book of Acts
87 Praise And The Power In Our Tongue
91 God's Laws for Healing
92 Monogamous Marriage Is Best
94 My Testimony

WHAT IS IT ALL ABOUT?

I read a story the other day about Jesus as a child. It described an incident that brought great excitement to a group of people. Jesus was just a small boy. A bird had died, and someone placed the dead bird in his hand. It came back to life and flew away!

Was this a true story? The Bible proves it was not. It clearly says Jesus did no miracles until after the Holy Spirit came from heaven and landed on Him, like a dove in appearance to those watching. He was being baptized in water when His Father sent Him down to endue Him with power.

So this means Jesus came to earth to become a human being, though He was part of the Godhead, leaving His power behind. Why? He is our example to follow, and this same power is available to us as His followers. After these baptisms, He was led to the desert and Satan, the fallen angel, confronted Him there, tempting Him to worship him!

When He returned after forty days of fasting, He began His miracle ministry. Why do you suppose God empowered Jesus to do miracles everywhere He went? Jesus once said, "If you don't believe Me because of who I claim to be, believe me then because of the miracles I do." These miracles are now done by God's Holy Spirit living in believers today.

Jesus is our example to follow. Just before He ascended into heaven on the mountain with 500 watching, He said He was sending His Spirit to them when He got to heaven. They were to wait for Him in Jerusalem. And up He went, into the clouds. I doubt it took long to get to heaven but it took a while for the Holy Spirit to come down for some reason

I wonder if it took a while for all the people to have enough united faith to receive Him? Or some gave up and went home. Out of all those witnesses, only 120 remained in an upper room in the city on that awesome day. It was during a feast day, and people from all over the known world were in the city.

Suddenly as they were praising God, a mighty wind entered the room, maybe like a tornado. Each person was astounded to see what looked like a flame on top of every head! And each of them started talking, but only a foreign language came out of each mouth!

They ran outside, maybe to see if there really was a tornado! They tried to tell people what happened, but all they could speak was this babble! The most amazing thing was that foreigners understood them! The Holy Spirit had His first chance to share the good news of Jesus' resurrection to the entire known world!

What is my point in writing? Do you see where you fit into this pattern? Jesus came from heaven and took on a human form to be a payment for the sins of mankind. The only condition to have sins forgiven and erased is that we believe what God has recorded in the Bible about it. Read John 3:16. God gave His only begotten son, that whoever will believe in Him shall not perish, but have everlasting life.

God required from the beginning of the world, after Adam committed the first sin, that sin could be forgiven if a perfect sacrifice was made and that sinless animal's blood would be shed as a payment for that sin. Millions of animals were killed, because man could not be perfect, no matter how hard he tried. Jesus would be the permanent perfect payment, because He was the only 'man' who never sinned.

Jesus is also our example on how God expects us to live on this earth. If we follow His teaching and imitate Him, we should be able to do the same things He did. He actually said, "You shall do even greater things than I, because I am going to the Father." He sent the Spirit down so we would have this same power. Can you imagine?

So how do we come to this point? We certainly need to study our Bibles to find out what He did and how He did it. He is our guide into a supernatural realm! Isn't that exciting? So far, in my life this has been true, but I want more.

When we get this revelation, yes, power manifests in our lives, but not without warfare. Satan is God's enemy, and of course ours as well. He is able to put thoughts in our minds. If we walk out from the umbrella of God's protection through obedience, he is also able to do other things to us. When God says He chastens us, all He has to do is let us reap what we sow.

Now the solution for that is repentance, meaning we ask forgiveness and turn around our lives to again obey God. We are again in a safe place, and able to help others find that place as well.

So…we read our Bible, we learn God's plan of salvation, we become born again with His spirit moving inside us, and we begin living like Jesus did on earth. We get baptized in water as a sign of our rebirth and our death to our old self, buried in the water.

Then we invite Jesus to baptize us with His Holy Spirit, and He endues us with the power to live as He lived. We share the good news, we heal the sick as Jesus did, we cast out evil spirits, and we give God all the praise and glory for it all! Life gets real exciting! I would not go back to my old life for anything!

YES, THERE IS A WAR GOING ON.

Have you thoughts ever disagreed with things God has said are true? Do you think more like God thinks now than you did five years ago? Is it difficult to get into studying the Bible? Do you ever have trouble sitting down to talk to the Lord?

Do you believe there is a literal devil and does he have an army of soldiers? When did the battle begin? Define battle: struggle, contest, controversy.

How can we fight someone we cannot see? How do we know he is present? How does the devil attack? If we cannot be lost, why would Satan torment us or try to lure us away from obeying God?

How can we be lost after we have accepted Jesus? What does the Bible say? So if it is possible for us to turn from God and reject His very existence, is it important to overcome or conquer this evil one who tries to torment us?

We have three enemies. What are they? World, flesh and devil. What armor and ammunition does God supply us with to win this war? What does the devil use that we need to resist? Defeat, discouragement, fear, stress, busyness, strife, division. Self-pity (which is based on pride; "I deserve better." Why do we deserve anything?)

We have weapons to use against all three.

Against the devil: Awareness. Ephesians 6: 11-18 armor to put on daily. Helmet, breastplate, belt, boots, sword, shield, and prayer. Rom 8:26

Praise breaks the yoke of bondage. Walls of Jericho came tumbling down. Praise opened prison doors. 2 Chron 20:22; Ps 22:3.

Agree with God. Eph 6:18; James 5:16; Study God's Book. Truth overcomes lies, but we must recognize the difference. 2 Tim 3:16

Against the flesh: Acts 1:8 We receive power when the Holy Spirit comes upon us. When we pray in a language the devil does not know what it is. God is praying for us in ways we do not even know needed praying for.

All prayer is good. Ask anything in My name and I will give it to you, according to My will. Ask largely that your joy may be full.

Does God hear our prayer if we are living in sin? Can Satan make us sin? Is temptation sin? How do we overcome temptation? Be armed with God's Word. Make no provision for the flesh. Depend on

Jesus life in you. See yourself as dead to sin and alive to Christ. Be careful to surround yourself with those that walk with Christ. Remain grateful for what Jesus did on the cross and does for you daily-meets all needs. Realize you have been given power over sin and you now know what it is. Romans 6:11,12.

"He who has died is freed from sin. The law of the Spirit of life in Jesus has made us free from the law of sin and death. Romans 8:2

Arm yourself: take the sword of the Spirit-word of God. Eph 6:17. When we walk in the spirit we will not fulfill the lust of the flesh. How do we walk in the spirit? We obey God. What does He tell us to do? Two things. Put Him first. Love neighbor as self. Fulfills them all.

I read "Tortured for Christ," by Richard Wurmbrand. How did he get so strong? 2 Cor 10:5 He forgave!

Against the world: and its beliefs, philosophies, lies, perversions. Rev 12:11 *They overcame with the blood of the Lamb and the word of their testimony. And they did not love their lives unto death.* If we try to save our lives we will lose them. If we are willing to loves our lives for His sake we will save them.

The joy of the Lord is our strength. Neh. 8:10 "Do not grieve. Enjoy choice food, sweet drinks and send some to those without. This day is holy to our Lord." Why rejoice? It is because we are forgiven, clean before God, free from punishment, safe, protected for all eternity. Our high priest intercedes for us all the time. His love is deeper than you can know.

Do not expect it to be all roses. In this world you will have tribulation. "Rejoice! I, Jesus, have overcome the world! You are more than conquerors through Me."

Get ready for the possibility that believers in America will be persecuted. There is power in numbers. There is comfort in unity. God is with us. He will never let us be tempted more than we can resist, either.

WHY PRAY? HOW to PRAY? WHEN to PRAY?

Prayer is the key that unlocks everything! Mark 11:[22] So Jesus answered and said to them, "Have faith in God. [23] For assuredly, I say to you, whoever says to this mountain, 'Be removed and be cast into the sea,' and does not doubt in his heart, but believes that those things he says will be done, he will have whatever he says. [24] Therefore I say to you, whatever things you ask when you pray, believe that you receive *them,* and you will have *them.*"

Forgiveness and Prayer

[25] "And whenever you stand praying, if you have anything against anyone, forgive him, that your Father in heaven may also forgive you your trespasses. [26] But if you do not forgive, neither will your Father in heaven forgive your trespasses."

Phillip. 4:[6] Be anxious for nothing, but in everything by prayer and supplication, with thanksgiving, let your requests be made known to God; [7] and the peace of God, which surpasses all understanding, will guard your hearts and minds through Christ Jesus.

Meditate on These Things

[8] Finally, brethren, whatever things are true, whatever things *are* noble, whatever things *are* just, whatever things *are* pure, whatever things *are* lovely, whatever things *are* of good report, if *there is* any virtue and if *there is* anything praiseworthy—meditate on these things.

Jer 33:3 Moreover the word of the LORD came to Jeremiah a second time, while he was still shut up in the court of the prison, saying, [2] "Thus says the LORD who made it, the LORD who formed it to establish it (the[a] LORD *is* His name): [3] 'Call to Me, and I will answer you, and show you great and [b]mighty things, which you do not know.'

Rom 12: I beseech[a] you therefore, brethren, by the mercies of God, that you present your bodies a living sacrifice, holy, acceptable to God, *which is* your [b]reasonable service. ² And do not be conformed to this world, but be transformed by the renewing of your mind, that you may prove what *is* that good and acceptable and perfect will of God.

If we have lost our faith we will not pray. Prayer is based on faith. Where do we get faith? God gives every man a gift of faith-a measure of faith. We may not all have the same measure but all have faith-enough to get saved. Jesus died to save all, not just some.

So how can we increase our faith? Read God's letters to us, His record of deeds, His promises, His warnings, His miracles, His history, His prophecies, His wisdom. All we need to live victoriously is in that one Book.

It helps to write down our thoughts when we are confused or being attacked by lies. Compare those thoughts with scripture.

Use a concordance if you like, and look up the subjects involved.

Man cannot live by bread/food alone, but by every word proceeding from the mouth of God. Matt 4:4

I am reading a profound book called "The Heavenly Man." Yun lives in China, and was a pastor. He was arrested for refusing to go to the Chinese church called the Three-self church, about communist propaganda.

The officials tortured him nearly every day trying to get him to give names of other believers and renounce Jesus. They used electric charges inside his mouth and everywhere, beat him, starved him and put him in a four foot box for months where he could not stretch or stand. His memorized verses kept him sane. Nothing else.

Near the end of his sentence, the other prisoners (who also hurt him and mocked him) came down with boils. He got none. They were determined to infect him and forced him to lie down on their clothing to catch the bugs. Nothing worked. At one point he fasted for 74 days! All that he suffered eventually worked on the other prisoners, and after the attacks on their bodies from more than one plague (that he didn't get) the whole prison got saved.

Prayer requires faith. If we had no faith, there would be no desire to pray. What is the point? We would not expect an answer!

The Lord's Prayer: Our Father in heaven, Hallowed be Your name.[10] Your kingdom come. Your will be done on earth as *it is* in heaven.[11] Give us this day our daily bread.[12] And forgive us our debts, As we forgive our debtors.[13] And do not lead us into temptation, But deliver us from the evil one.[a] For Yours is the kingdom and the power and the glory forever. Amen.

God answers those that diligently seek Him. So when we feel we don't even know any more how to pray, a good place to start is by praising. Set your mind to see the glass half full and not half empty. Focus on blessings.

Or begin with the Lord's Prayer. Or put on praise music and just think about His attributes before speaking.

When you pray, think on these things, all that is worthy and of good report. Think about life before you knew God and how thankful you are to have been chosen for His kingdom. What changed since you came into His grace and favor?

What do you now have you are thankful for? What are you struggling with that you need help?

Pour out your heart as though you were sitting in front of a counselor who is asking what is going on with your life? What bothers you? What feelings are you dealing with? What do you want God to do for you? Consider that nothing is impossible with Him. You may ask anything according to His will. Then you must fight the good fight of faith and determine to trust Him for it. Encourage the angels with your gratitude to God. Repeat back to God His promises, not so He knows, but He knows you know. Claim them. Thank Him ahead of time for answering. Then after prayer be sure to speak only faith that He will fulfill them. A double minded person will get no answers from Him.

Wait on the Lord and renew your strength and mount up with wings as eagles!

So why do we pray? When? How? To commune with Him and know Him better. Without ceasing. With praise, petition, thanks.

Be sure to record your prayers and your answers. God said to remember the things He has done for you. It helps greatly when you need encouragement.

WHY MIRACLES?

Why is it important to believe in miracles? What prevents us from receiving one? How do we obtain one?

Why do so many today become Christians when they see or experience a miracle? Are they still important? A member of my family is bedridden with MS. I believe in miracles and write books on my experiences with supernatural events! How can I help her receive one? I hope this article will help.

Where do we begin? Since the world began, God did not plan for us to die. But when Adam and Eve accepted Satan's accusation of God by disobeying Him, death came to all descendants. What would the world be like if Eve had stood up for God? She could have said, "Yes, that is what God said! I believe God!" Sin was born.

God arranged to forgive sins, using blood as payment, but it was temporary. He would forgive the sin if the person killed an animal and poured its blood on an altar. Millions of innocent animals have died due to the sin of breaking God's laws.

Here is the foundation of Christianity. God is a triune being, like an egg is three parts but one egg. God the Son, Jesus, came to earth from heaven as a seed inside Mary, as a human being (but also God the Son) to show the way to heaven and become a permanent blood payment for sin to all that will believe. He grew up, taught the world about God and His ways and demonstrated God's love by doing miracles.

Jesus' entire ministry was based on miracles. Why did He do so many miracles? Why did He turn water into wine? Feed 5000 hungry people? Heal everyone who came to Him?

When Jesus was asked to prove who He was, He said, "If you don't believe what I say, then believe because of the miracles I do!"

Jesus said those are His who trust Him and believe in Him. So first we must be born again. Many have never heard that term. Begin with John 3:16 and go through the Romans Road Romans 3:23; 6:23; 10:9,10. Jesus said you must be born again to enter the kingdom of God. Jesus is the bridge that connects us to Father God. He was a perfect Lamb who never sinned. He agreed to die in our place and shed His blood for all who will believe in Him. All we need to do is thank Jesus and invite Him to take over our lives. We will belong to Him forever as His children.

Jesus not only allowed Himself to be killed on the cross but allowed His body to be beaten, beyond recognition as a human being! He could have called ten thousand angels! He didn't. God said we are healed from sickness because Jesus took upon Himself all the sickness of the world and "by His stripes we were healed," if we accept it. So salvation is a gift of <u>eternal life and freedom from sickness</u>! Hang on. You will catch it soon. I have lots more evidence.

Now we are <u>members</u> of the Kingdom of God. We have certain rights and have inherited many things.

God also did not plan for sickness to attack us. Satan is the source of such curses. *Satan comes to steal, kill and destroy us, but Jesus came that we might have an abundant life.* See John 10:10.

Now we know we are going to heaven; our sins are forgiven, past, present and even future. We know where sickness came from. We know Jesus made provision for our healing by faith in Him.

So <u>faith</u> is the currency of the kingdom! How much currency do you have? How do you get that? Jesus gave every human the measure of faith. Romans 12:3. So we all have faith as a gift. We must exercise it to give it strength, like muscles. We must know this faith is based on the Bible. If you ever study the origin of our Bible, it will astound you! Believe me; you can trust it with your life! God wrote the Bible, using human hands to give it substance here. He told people what to write and they obeyed.

Faith increases by hearing over and over the <u>Word of Truth</u>. We digest it, memorize it, speak it aloud, and choose to believe it. God gives free will. We can decide what to believe. If you want a miracle, I would suggest scriptures.

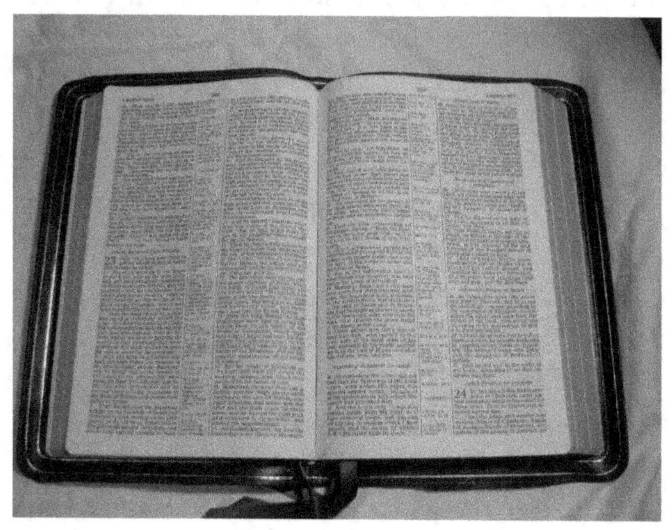

Nearly every page in the Bible records a <u>miracle</u>. It is not over as some try to tell us! Where do they come up with such nonsense? God is the same today, yesterday and FOREVER! Jesus even said we would do greater things than He did! John 14:12.

I would suggest if you are seeking a miracle that you sit under this sort of teaching three times before you go forward for someone to put their hands on you to receive it. This way you will be prepared, forearmed and filled with faith, with no doubts. And your miracle will begin to manifest in your life.

Consider your salvation. You believed the good news. You thanked Jesus and invited Him to take your life and have His way with you. Then you went home and the battle began. Right? I wonder how many have prayed the prayer and got attacked by Satan and his horde of lying spirits and just walked away?

The same thing happens when you come and ask Jesus to heal you. Be prepared for the onslaught. Here are a few of Satan's tactics. Jesus warned us. He said we must tear down strongholds in our minds and transform our minds into the mind of Jesus, thinking like He thinks.

Some are simply ignorant of what the Bible says. Remember when Jesus got baptized and the Holy Spirit came and immersed Him with power? He went to the desert where Satan tempted Him. Good thing to study over. How did Jesus shut him up? "Satan, it is written…" He used scriptures to shut his mouth and it worked! God has the final word. Ephesians 6:10+

describes our armor against evil spirits. Read it and get armed every day.

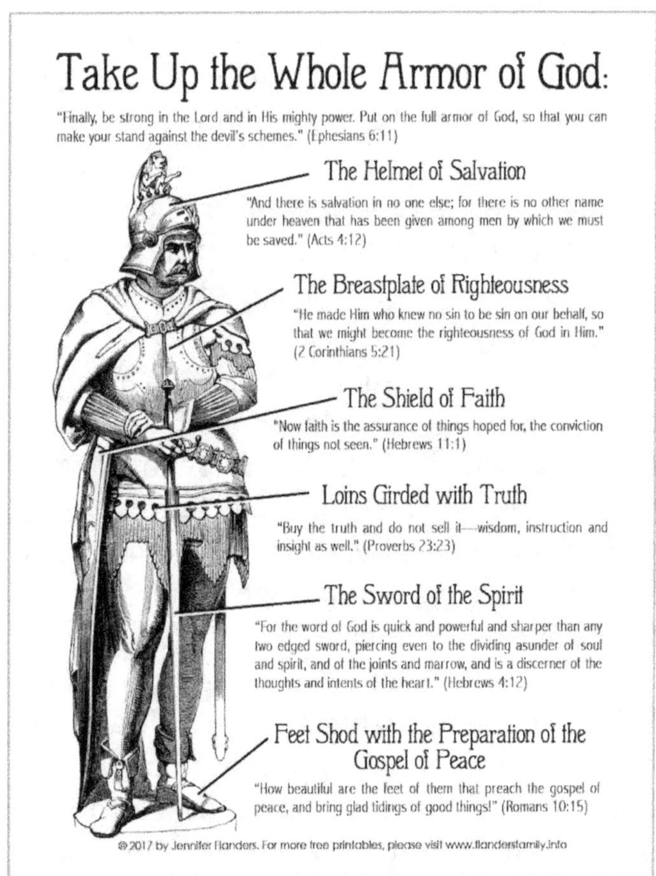

Some of us have trusted people instead of God to teach us their views.

Always discern what you hear with the Word. For example: all cults reject Christ as their Savior, even if everything else lines up with scripture. In these last days there is much deception, even from good leaders. God said never to put your trust in man…and that even includes doctors, smarter than us, but human. Be careful not to accept a doctor's diagnosis and tell it out loud. Life and death is in the power of our tongue. If we accept his diagnosis instead of speaking what God said, those words are empowered.

I had a friend who received a doctor's report that she would die of cancer. She told him, "I will live and not die, and I will declare the works of the Lord." She did not die, and next time he checked her, the cancer was gone! My pastor's wife did the same. The breast lump had disappeared when they opened her up.

What other strongholds block us from receiving by faith? One is unforgiveness. God said if we refuse to forgive our enemies, God won't forgive our sins! That is heavy! Matthew 6:14-15. A root of bitterness defiles not only that person but others as well.

James 1:7 tells us that a doubleminded person receives nothing from God. What does that mean? Doubts? About the Bible? About His ability to heal? His desire to heal us all? If we think He is picking and choosing, how can we not doubt whether it will be us? Some say, "God will heal me if it is His will." If we cannot have doubts, that statement shoots us in the water!

What about expecting healing, but continuing a sin-filled life? Yes, God forgives, but He also expects change in our lives once we recognize it as sin! He has revealed it and empowers us to quit! Does He have the right to expect us to at least repent and do our best to be obedient? Repent means to reconsider, be sorry, regret, turn back, and to return. Ask Him!

We must know our own heart. Some fear a loss if they get healed. Deep down they avoid healing, fearing a loss of government money, sympathy, attention, caretakers and other things. Sometimes sickness has its own reward system we need to recognize and decide about.

Consider the woman with the issue of blood. She had spent all she had on doctors. She had no recourse. She had to go in public where they had the legal right to stone her for coming out in that condition. But in desperation she grabbed Jesus' garment and power left Him! He said, "Your faith has healed you."

You must be totally convinced God wants you well no matter what. How do you obtain your miracle? If you are sick, James says to call on the elders (if they believe!) and let them anoint you with oil, the symbol of the Holy Spirit.

That is not the only way to pray. God also says if two or more agree in prayer, the prayer of faith will heal the person. Remember when Jesus prayed for the dead child, He first removed all unbelievers from the room. Important.

Sometimes there is a spirit that influences a person; even a Christian can be controlled by an evil spirit. Their spirit is protected, but the body or mind can be affected. My friend had cancer; it was conquered but came back. She was so discouraged she decided just to let it take her life. Her husband found out and brought her to a pastor, who discerned it was a spirit. They fasted before meeting because some only come out with prayer and fasting. The pastor cast it out. She was immediately healed! No medical intervention was used.

Going to conferences or meetings where miracles are happening helps our faith leap! God has given us many spiritual gifts when we ask Him to baptize us with His Holy Spirit, and one of them is a special gift of healing. Other gifts help too, like the gift of miracles or a special gift of faith.

So: we get saved, we ask for the Holy Spirit baptism and the gifts that come with it, we forgive, we change our mind about incorrect beliefs, we overcome every doubt, and then we ask God to meet our need. Mark 11:24 says to ask, believe we receive, and then we get it. So we thank Him before receiving it.

We hold onto our confession of faith no matter what symptoms remain, we stand firm, we overcome attacks by speaking

God's promises aloud, and the miracle comes about. Then we overcome by the word of our testimony and the blood of the Lamb. Rev.12:11. Hold on tight to what you believe. It will manifest.

God does not tempt us, but He does let us be tested sometimes. So we wait and fight the good fight of faith until we receive what He promised and paid for. God promised to meet all our needs through Christ Jesus and His riches in glory! If we are desperate enough to put God first in our lives, seek Him with a whole heart, we will be found of Him, and He will give us our hearts' desire! Enjoy your new life!

Find Those That Manifest Gifts

According to a book by John G. Lake, Jesus' methods of healing are scientific. Science is really the discovery of how God does things. Healing is based on the law of contact and transmission. The Spirit emanates from a touch. The authority in the name of Jesus is all that is needed when we are baptized with the Holy Spirit and we believe with a whole heart; there can be no doubting. That is one reason often we go to a person that has the spiritual gift of faith, or gift of healing or the gift of miracles, specifically for that purpose. Their faith plus our own faith with produce what we seek.

The Spirit of God is a tangible substance, a heavenly materiality. It is capable of being stored even in cloth as in the garments of Jesus and the handkerchiefs of Paul.

We received Jesus into our hearts as a response to His love, His offer of eternal life in exchange for a simple act of faith, that what He did and said is true!

Not all miracles or healings occur instantly. The lepers were healed as they went. When Jesus laid His hands on the blind man, first he could only see men as trees. Even Jesus had to lay His hands on him a second time for his healing to be complete.

The miracle realm is natural once we enter God's kingdom. He said we are not of this world once we give our lives to Him. We live under different rules, and are under God's mercy and grace.

When we live as sinners, our mind dominates our lives. When we are born again, our spirit takes dominion. Miracles become our basic nature. No more self-centered living, no more a self-seeking human. We are new creatures in Christ Jesus. God's Spirit in us restrains us from sinning as He molds us into the image of Christ.

Man's intellect is conscious of supernatural forces he cannot understand. The knowledge of God is written on the heart of every man. Once he surrenders to God, he can be released from self and the sin nature that cannot behave.

God says to seek Him with all our hearts and we will be found of Him.

Healing is but a means to an end. The object is health of body, soul and spirit. Altogether they complete the union of man with God when the Holy Spirit possesses it all.

Jesus paid for our souls on the cross. He paid for our healing by taking the stripes. There are 39 major disease groups and He took 39 stripes!

When we transform our minds into the mind of Christ, God's Word will overcome every stronghold in our mind. When all doubts are conquered, healing will come. God is willing to respond to our faith. As we speak aloud God's word, faith grows- from hearing His Word.

Why Hide the Word?

God said we are to hide His Word in our hearts. How do we do that? Read it, dissect it, look up hidden meanings, memorize it, believe it and speak it.

Words are our very life! God said to believe in our heart that Jesus is the Christ, the Son of the living God, and confess it with our mouth.

We overcome sickness with the Word. God said He sent His Word and healed them/us. We can also prevent sickness with the Word. God said we are to be anxious for nothing. 80% of all sickness is said to be caused by stress or anxiety. He also said life and death is in the power of the tongue. When we speak God's living Word we empower our bodies to fall in line with His promises. God created the world with words, and He lives inside us! By our words we are justified or we are condemned.

We can deliver people from evil spirits with words! Jesus gave us all authority over them, using His name as a cop would by saying, "Stop, in the name of the law!". The devil came to steal, kill and destroy, but Jesus came to give us a more abundant life. He said His people perish for lack of knowledge. When we find out what the Bible really says, we do not perish but have everlasting life.

It is all ours once we see it in the 'contract!' The New Testament is Jesus' last will and testament, our inheritance!

We stand in faith to overcome the battles in our mind. We tear down strongholds in our mind and transform our minds into the mind of Christ.

Mark 5:25-34 The Passion Translation (TPT) *[25] Now, in the crowd that day was a woman who had suffered horribly from continual bleeding for twelve years.[a] [26] She had endured a great deal under the care of various doctors, yet in spite of spending all she had on their treatments, she was not getting better, but worse. [27] When she heard about Jesus' healing power, she pushed through the crowd and came up from behind him and touched his prayer shawl.[b]*

28 For she kept saying to herself, "If only I could touch his clothes, I know I will be healed."[c] 29 As soon as her hand touched him, her bleeding immediately stopped! She knew it, for she could feel her body instantly being healed of her disease!30 Jesus knew at once that someone had touched him, for he felt the power that always surged around him[d] had passed through him for someone to be healed. He turned and spoke to the crowd, saying, "Who touched my clothes?"[e]31 His disciples answered, "What do you mean, who touched you? Look at this huge crowd—they're all pressing up against you." 32 But Jesus' eyes swept across the crowd, looking for the one who had touched him for healing.33 When the woman who experienced this miracle[f] realized what had happened to her, she came before him, trembling with fear, and threw herself down at his feet, saying, "I was the one who touched you." And she told him her story of what had just happened.34 Then Jesus said to her, "Daughter, because you dared to believe, your faith has healed you. Go with peace in your heart, and be free from your suffering!"

When this sinks in, your life will be transformed! You have heard it for years and it sounds real nice, but believing it will change everything! God said if we confess with our mouth and believe with our heart that Jesus is Lord we will be saved.

In the Old Testament twelve spies went to Canaan, the land God promised to give them. When they saw the giants, ten of them came home saying, "We cannot overcome those giants! We cannot take the land!" They must have been devastated! They were depending on their own strength. Only two believed and said they could take the land; and they did. Those that said no spent forty years in that desert as a result! What do you suffer as a result of words you have spoken? By our words we are justified and by our words we are condemned. We gotta pay attention to our mouth! It has great power! God created the world with words and He lives inside us!

People ask, "Why can't I be healed?" Do you see why? They are speaking unbelief right there. They just spoke it. Hope is not faith. Faith is stronger, and manifests in our words. Wrong thinking, wrong believing and wrong talking puts us in bondage. We need to repent and ask God to erase those confessions and forgive us. Then we can start with a clean slate.

Consider concerns about getting old. Many older people fear getting dementia or Alzheimer's disease. We often talk about it and try to encourage each other that we won't get it. But words pop out giving power to our fear. We must repent and start over. We don't have to admit we are forgetting more as time goes on. We don't have to. Moses didn't. He was strong in every way to the end of his life.

Our mind never ages. It operates using our brain. They are two different things. We have the mind of Christ. He tells us to transform our minds into the mind of Christ. We must not prepare for failure but for success. A well-known speaker claims that only three out of a hundred men actually succeed in doing what they planned to accomplish in life. That is not a great number. This may be the reason. We must not prepare for failure but for success.

Kenneth Hagin was an invalid due to heart problems, and given one in a million chances of even staying alive past sixteen. He caught this vision and began meditating on this profound truth. Seven months later, after fighting the good fight of faith against the devil, he put on shoes and walked all the way to town, weeping with joy! He never stopped! He became a powerful preacher in the Baptist church. Then he discovered the baptism with the Holy Spirit and began to heal thousands in the name of Jesus!

What is it you lack in your life? What do you want? Of course it must line up with God's will. "Ask anything in line with His will and you may have it." *Matthew 7:7-8 The Passion Translation (TPT)[7] "Ask, and the gift is yours. Seek, and you'll discover. Knock, and the door will be opened for you. [8] For every persistent one will get what he asks for. Every persistent seeker will discover what he longs for. And everyone who knocks persistently will one day find an open door.[a]* **1 John 5:14** *Since we have this confidence, we can also have great boldness before him, for if we present any request agreeable to his will, he will hear us.*

Matthew 18:19 *Again, I give you an eternal truth: If two of you agree to ask God for something in a symphony of prayer,[a] my heavenly Father will do it for you.*

Matthew 21:22 *Everything you pray for with the fullness of faith you will receive!"[a]* John 14:13 *For I will do whatever you ask me to do when you ask me in my name. And that is how the Son will show what the Father is really like and bring glory to him.*

My People Perish for Lack of Knowledge

God gives great wisdom about alcohol. It is the reason for 80% of suicide victims. It poisons every organ. Eph 5:17-18 *Don't be a fool. Realize God doesn't want you to waste your life drunk on alcoholic spirits. Instead be filled with the Holy Spirit.* Check Proverbs 23.

What does God say about cancer? 120,000 a year die from lung cancer from smoking, resulting in 300 funerals a day in America. It causes emphysema, wrinkles, sterility, second-hand diseases, the unborn are shorter, sicker and less intelligent. 80% start smoking before age sixteen!

Is circumcision good or bad? Muslims do it to girls! They believe it will keep them safe from going after sex. They also stitch up her womb-usually without numbing! At around the age of five!! This is insane!

85% of men in America get circumcised today. A man considered it barbaric and tried to reverse it. Yuck. He started a support group called RECA. The uncircumcized contract eight times more AIDS than those with a circumcision.

Sex IN marriage is a great protection, especially if both get tested before marriage for diseases. None of the Jews got cancer. They are also safer from urinary tract infections. Testing from 1971 to 1989 proved the benefits greatly outweighed any risk.

Boys in the Bible were circumcised on the eighth day after birth. This is proven to be the day with the least risk of bleeding. God planned it that way. Vitamin K is the highest at that time. Now they give a shot of Vitamin K and do it usually on the third day after birth. Babies heal much faster than older children. Gen.17:12

God said to use a NEW flint knife. He was specific. It would be free of germs even then.

Born Gay? No such thing! They keep trying to prove it but have no evidence that God made such a horrendous mistake!

Identical twins who share the same gene structure would both be gay then, but they are not. It is a result of different experiences. The majority of people were molested as children and got confused.

A sad story- a mother decided to make her daughter into a boy at age five, cut her hair, dressed her as a boy and told her she is a boy. She enrolled her in school as a boy. She uses the boy's bathroom, but wants to be a girl! The judge is on the divorced mother's side against the father's protests!

Homosexual hunters are out there tempting. They often use drugs or alcohol to dull the normal senses and the conscience. They reduce inhibitions that protect us. Their goal is money, enslavement, destruction, sexual "thrill", variety, and to reduce the sense of right and wrong.

Thirty percent of the men in prison are reported to practice it. Most quit when they get out and live as normal people. It is not what they are or were. It is just what they do or did. 80% of gay men were distant from their fathers! A loving father is a vaccination against homosexuality. Eph. 6:4. Smothering mothers can pressure and drive boys from females as well. Sex is a gift from God in a moral setting and within His boundaries. Ex.15:26 *"If you diligently heed the voice of the LORD your God and do what is right in His sight, give ear to His commandments and keep all His statutes, I will put none of the diseases on you which I have brought on the Egyptians. For I am the LORD who heals you."*

Thirty percent of gays are reported to have about a thousand partners! 100% are unfaithful within five years!

90% of AIDS is spread by heterosexuals! In Africa ten million children were orphaned by AIDS in the year 2000.

Beware of STD's (sexually transmitted diseases): Before marriage if you are going to marry-get tested! Do not have sex before marriage! It will certainly have a negative effect- assured. 30% of young adults carry the HPV-venereal warts that cause cervical cancer.

PID (Pelvic inflammatory disease) is the major cause of infertility. 1:20 cases. Prov.5:1-9.

My son, do not forget my law, But let your heart keep my commands; [2] *For length of days and long life And peace they will add to you.* [3] *Let not mercy and truth forsake you; Bind them around your neck, Write them on the tablet of your heart,* [4] *And so find favor and [a] high esteem in the sight of God and man.*

[5] *Trust in the* LORD *with all your heart, And lean not on your own understanding;* [6] *In all your ways acknowledge Him, And He shall [b] direct your paths.*

[7] *Do not be wise in your own eyes; Fear the* LORD *and depart from evil.* [8] *It will be health to your [c] flesh, And strength[d] to your bones.*

Sex facts: Women want intimacy. Men want pleasure. Women are in control of lust more than men. Heb. 13:4 *Marriage is honorable among all, and the bed undefiled; but fornicators and adulterers God will judge.* [5] *Let your conduct be without covetousness; be content with such things as you have. For He Himself has said, "I will never leave you nor forsake you."*

Saving the sexual experience for marriage protects the heart- in every way! In the early 1900's, 97.5% were virgins at marriage. Today 40% of high school boys have had sex with at least four girls. Liberated women? NO! Women are trapped, in bondage. JUST SAY NO!

If a man wants sex before marriage, and leaves if you refuse, this is good riddance. He will do it to you after marriage in many cases. "No" gives you power and peace! You can choose to be a victor or a victim.

What is Repentance?

Matthew 3: Produce fruit in keeping with repentance. 11: (John said) I baptize you with water for repentance. But after me comes one who is more powerful than I, whose sandals I am not worthy to carry. He will baptize you with the Holy Spirit and fire.

Mathew 9:13 Go and learn what this means: "I desire mercy, not sacrifice. For I have not come to call the righteous but sinners." (Jesus)

Acts 5:31 God exalted Jesus to His own right hand as Prince and Savior that He might bring Israel to repentance and forgive their sins.

Acts 11:17-18: So if God gave them the same gift He gave us who believed in the Lord Jesus Christ, who was I to think that I could stand in God's way? When they heard this, they had no further objections and praised God, saying, "So then, even to Gentiles God has granted repentance that leads to life."

To repent means to turn around and go the other way. Stop doing what you were doing, apologize to God and go His way.

We Are All Worshippers

We were created for this purpose. We were made to glorify God. He has a right to expect us to put Him first in our lives. The more we surrender ourselves to Him, reckon ourselves dead to sin and alive to God, the more He pours out His joy into us. That emotion is so contagious! Wherever we go, we get back smiles, love and acceptance. Life is good!

So what do I think about most? What gets my attention more than anything? This is a form of worship, to give your attention to something. When I first discovered Jesus was real, I was so enamored with His presence, I thought of nothing else all day long. Every day was spent first studying His word, singing with praise music and praying. He was so close! When I entered the church, His presence almost knocked me over! What has changed?

Then we come up with the enemy. The honeymoon period is over. Now for the conflict. What did Lucifer (Satan) want more than anything? Worship!

So forty-seven years later, what do I do with my day? I play with my dog, read a verse or one page of scripture, and get on my computer to visit with friends or write a book…about God's miracles! I repent.

God laid out a path to come close to Him. We are to enter His gates with thanksgiving, enter His courts with praise and come to the Holy of Holies with worship, adoration for who He is.

How do we manifest our worship? What comes first in our lives? Do we spend most of our time on our appearance? We exercise a lot, shop for clothes, get our nails and hair done perfectly, have friends over that build us up, and feel fulfilled and happy. But are we?

What do you spend the most time on? Movies? Books? Sports? Fixing cars? Petting and walking the dog? Cleaning house? Working to get rich?

If we have never entered the Holy of Holies, we have not yet experienced the greatest moment of our lives! If we have and we drifted off, we know what we are missing but can't seem to find our way back! Jesus warned about these times of losing our first love. It will take surrender, determination and desire to find that sweet spot again. But it is worth everything!

Our world is about to experience an outpouring of God's spirit and we need to be ready to receive them, and offer them salvation-which includes healing, deliverance, eternal life and prosperity. I will ask for His help and follow the path that leads to His heart. I'll let you know how it turns out.

What is a soul tie?

Soul invaders affect everyone. There are many references to them, using various terms.

Go to I Thes 5:23. We are three part beings. God is one God but He also has three parts. Jews disagree about Jesus because of the verse that says God is one God. I John 5:7 explains it further.

Our spirits are sealed and safe. Eph. 1:13. God takes us through a sanctification process. He sets us apart and changes us into the image of Jesus over time, as the Word becomes part of us. That is why He said to meditate on the Word. Chew it up and digest it.

God wants our mind renewed. The spirit is new. Now the mind and body should follow. Then we will fulfill the purpose we were created for.

God tells us to renew our mind. He says to tear down strongholds. How can we, if we don't even know they exist?

Psalm 23 talks of our soul being restored. From what to what?

Without peace no one shall see God. We need to know how to achieve peace no matter what goes on around us.

Heb. 11 says we are to seek Him with all our heart. Then He will find us.

The word 'soulties' is not in the Bible but references are.

We are connected to others in various ways. We have biological soulties with family.

Emotional ties with friends, loved ones

Sexual soulties with a spouse. Only one is allowed. Any more have to be broken and cast out of us. They cause many problems.

A lady stayed with an unfaithful husband for years. He would leave for weeks at a time and return. Counselor said she had grounds to separate. She told about her druggie dad who after years because she never gave up, got saved before he died. She stuck by the husband in hopes of saving him. Finally he got saved, and the marriage got built solid. It was a high price but worth it. She kept forgiving over and over. Hard.

Verbal ties- agreements we make- hope they are good

Mental ties- again, agreeing with the beliefs of others ties us together-good or bad.

Spiritual ties-church family, or in case of evil ties, consider when God warned His people not to associate with the heathen nations around them. They created evil soul ties and made God jealous-started giving credit to other gods.

The Bible uses words like cleave, knit, partake, join, be in one accord, and yoked. You know these terms. Slang today is "hookup" but that does not sound like a good soultie!

Ties with demons are the kind that need to be broken, but first we need to know they exist! There are many symptoms. One is that we have no peace and our joy is gone.

Why? Who or what did we join with in some way?

There is such a thing as a Jezebel spirit. It cannot be seen but it is real, and can alter your life. It is controlling and manipulative, like the one in the Bible, who made people sacrifice their children!

Incubus is a sexual spirit that came into a person who asked for it, just being funny and not believing it was real. It did sexual things to her, and after a time it came into her room and actually beat her! Never ask for a spirit!

There are websites that lure you to do just that. Uninformed people play with it and end up needing deliverance to get rid of it! Beware! One is called Momo. Drugs involve spirits. That is why Satan lures kids with drugs. Demons have freedom to take over their minds. Run the other way!

God has soulties with man that are good. John 170-21; Romans 10:9,10; Acts 2:1

Offenses open us up to ungodly soulties. That is why God said to forgive everyone-for your own protection! If not, demons have legal rights to torment you.

Soul ties involve your mind (thoughts, including subconscious ones)

They involve your will (reasoning, intellect) and your emotions (instinct, intuition) and your conscience, which is God's truth in us.

Romans 1 says the knowledge of God is written on every heart, so if someone is an atheist, it is simply because he has resisted God to where he denies His existence.

Jonathan and King David had soulties of brotherly love. It was good. They were loyal friends.

David and Saul had bad ones. Saul got jealous of David and kept trying to kill him. They started out with Saul being happy with him. He played music and soothed Saul when he was upset.

John 13:34-35 Love one another. This is God's command. Knit together with agape love.

WALKING WITH JESUS

May 3, 1980: I took my friend Val to FGBMF and heard Bill Basanski. Wow! What a testimony! Jesus was there! He told about the 66 million deaths in Russian labor camps in the early 1900's. Six million Jews sounds small! Seventeen million people are in Siberia and 15% die every day! Of two thousand people escaping a town, ten-year-old Bill and his family were the only family who survived. As they fled the town planes shot at their group and the shots went all around them, and not one hit them. The rest were frozen in mud/blood pools! Jesus later healed his paralysis of fourteen years duration at a Kathryn Kuhlman Crusade. Jesus manifested gifts of healing, discernment, words of knowledge and wisdom, and many were healed!

Madeline Murray O'Hare's son just confessed a belief in God! She was in the Roe v Wade trial of 1973 that resulted in legalized abortion on demand. Her son is trying to restore prayer in schools! Ironic.

It is important to accept people where they are at, loving them, even if they don't change. Give them the freedom to change. That includes family.

My friend Lynne was taught surgery is God's will. I brought her to Emory Hospital for it, and we prayed. She is in God's hands. She had one duct removed for biopsy. Later, while she waited for surgery, I poured a whole cup of olive oil on her chest and we prayed…didn't know any better! I had never seen anyone anointed before but read about it in James 5. God healed her and surgery was cancelled!

Wendy W. was healed of a massive chest tumor! The doctors read the body scans and agreed to surgery as crucial. All three saw it had disappeared! Peg saw three times the picture in her mind that I saw, that of Jesus in the waiting room, walking to Wendy and removing something from her chest!

July 15: Home safe and sound from Michigan. Rog drove the Herman Miller semi-truck and I followed, praying! The Lord protected him from a terrible accident! He was in the left lane and a driver called on the CB. "Herman Miller! Get in the right lane or you will be taking some barrels with you!" Rog just turned and there they were! PTL!

Dave, our oldest son, cut his finger and felt he needed stitches before we left. He fell over an electric cord and hurt his back and got a brace. Then he passed out from heat prostration due to hyperventilating form the brace. Last week he cut his head on the camper. A month ago he cut his foot in a river and had stitches. Before that he damaged his back again. What is this about? He may have a spirit of what? Infirmity? When we moved to Georgia from Michigan. He got an electrical shock and fell. He had surgery for a cyst, had a cycle accident, lost a tooth cap and got a root canal, and many other problems relating to health. The enemy torments this poor guy!

September 27: Our middle son Tom and youngest Rob got baptized! It was precious. What a precious child he turned out to be! He works hard at school, and so does Tom.

October 24: "*You need not believe Me for an instantaneous miracle of healing, but if you would preach it you must also walk in what you preach or risk being called a 'fake.' I will honor your effort to take only a day at a time by faith for a gradual healing. It is still My hand that stays the temptation and gives you power over it. If your faith wavers even an instant you must again stand firm. I shall give you the freedom again to choose correctly, even in a room filled with temptation. You will receive power to be unaffected if you begin to walk forward, one step, one foot at a time.*

Matthew 24 overview: signs of Christ's return: many will come in My name, lead astray, wars, rumors of war, nations fighting, famines, earthquakes, we will be delivered up to tribulation, hated, fall away, betray each other, false prophets, love cold, gospel preached through the world. Then the end will come. Sun goes dark. Stars fall. Moon goes dark. Powers of heaven are shaken. Sign of Jesus in heaven. All mourn. Then we see Jesus coming! Trumpet call. Gathers the elect! Be ready! Yesterday we had a meteor shower!

Our pastor Fred Kelly's mom had bladder cancer a long time. Last week she called Fred crying. The doctor will give her only a few days to live unless her bladder is removed! Fred flew home. When he arrived, five doctors had taken more tests and found the cancer had disappeared! They sent her home healed! God is so great!

May 4: Jeanette Kelly, his wife, is in the hospital with a fast growing breast tumor! They are doing a biopsy. Believing God is an active verb! (Later God healed her and surgery was cancelled.)

Astronaut Charles Duke spoke at *FGBMF! He said the moon was so peaceful. He never felt so free! I figure demons don't go that far away!

June 1: I ran out of gas at Toco Hills with Rob. Chugged to the station that "happened" to be 100 yards away! Miracle! Hard to find diesel fuel and Gulf so close.

Bob Johnson prophesied over me and God gave me: "Your children shall be taught of the Lord. Great shall be the wisdom of your children. You are about to launch into ministry. The foundations have been laid. You shall not go to the left or right but shall walk my narrow path. Tradition has taught

*Full Gospel Businessman's Fellowship

you that my narrow path is a difficult way but the truth is that my yoke is easy. My way is freedom. You shall speak the word of faith over your children and not doubt. Your family shall be walking in my spirit and great shall be their faithfulness. Study my word. Continue in my path. You have walked with me and in me, and in me you shall have your strength and your being. Rejoice in me. You shall have a freedom in my spirit as never before. Many are called, but few are chosen. I have chosen you."

That night Gail Solomon spoke over me as well. "You shall not veer to left or right but in my narrow way. You don't need to look to men for counsel for my spirit will direct you and will not lead you in a wrong path. He will show you the way to go. He has a perfect path for you to tread and he will reveal it to you."

I woke up with this lesson from the Holy Spirit. It is now November 30, 2016.

"Warn them before it is too late. The road is wide that leads to destruction. Narrow is the way that leads to life.

In the end times, many will fall away. They will follow teachers that preach about a different Jesus. Some will have itching ears. They will not endure sound doctrine, but will follow what appears to be a way that leads to life eternal, but this is not the way. Soon it will be too late to turn back. If you do not warn them, even at the risk of your relationship, I will hold you responsible because you did not tell them the truth.

You cannot have it both ways. You cannot have a loving relationship without truth. Love and truth are sisters. I will uphold you even in danger if you tell the truth. Tell about the benefits of that narrow path. "Pilgrim's Progress" is a good book for grandchildren at Christmastime. Teach them when they are young and they will escape many sorrows.

Truth cries out in the streets. Most will not listen but will mock the truth. If even one can be saved from hell, it is worth it. You are a voice in a wilderness of sin. It runs rampant, and will soon be as Sodom or Gomorrah. I have said, "Will I find faith on earth when I return?" It depends on my people doing what I called them to do.

Sowing and reaping can be good as well as bad. Try sowing the Word of God and you will reap a harvest."

Confirmation: Matthew 7:13; 24:10; I Tim 4:1; Mark 13:22; 2 Thess 2:1-12; Acts

20:29; 2 Cor 11:13-15; Eph 6:12; 2 Cor 11:3; 2 Peter 2:1-3,18,20

GREATER THAN LOVE?
(There is nothing greater.)

There is a power that appears to be greater than love. This power is destructive, evil, and overwhelming. Once a person gets a taste of it, he will literally sell his soul for it. He will do anything to get it, to the point of stealing, lying and manipulating.

It is so enticing, once it is experienced, a person will go to unbelievable lengths to get it and hold onto it. If anyone interferes or stands in the way, he appears to be the enemy. The real enemy is undercover, hiding under a disguise that is nearly invisible.

Oh, yes, once a person gets caught using this power, and threatened, he will agree to anything. But deep down, he has no intention of leaving this power alone. He will do anything to keep it.

If you love that person and try to help them get away from this magnetic force, you will be considered the enemy, though you are motivated only by love for that person.

This power messes up their perception of right and wrong. It alters their motives and changes them completely. Their brain activity even changes. They think differently. Their life focus is on one thing. "I gotta have another fix. Then life will be good again." But it is all a lie. Cocaine and heroin have no lasting benefit. They are not beneficial at all. They simply stimulate an area in the brain and body that feels good for a short time. Then comes the crash. But the brain says it is worth everything. It becomes a god unlike any other god.

This form of worship brings a person down to the bottom of the life pit. They are willing to sell everything they have for it. They will risk their very lives to get it. It has no value to the normal person. It makes no sense at all to one who has never experienced its effects. But for the one who has, it is the most valuable item that exists on the globe.

So what do you do if this person is someone you love? You can try to get through to them, to give alternatives, to bribe them to stop, to persuade them. It is all a waste of energy.

All you can do is let them fall to the bottom of the pit where they have no resources to go after more, and withdrawal begins. They can be locked up away from it, but even then they simply endure the separation until they are again free to get more.

Even God can't pour His love on them enough to give it up and come under His care! Their brain is already damaged. He certainly has the power to heal it, and give them sanity again if they would just ask

Him. Most end up dead or in prison for the things they have done to get hold of more. All this for a feeling! To a sane person it makes no sense. To one who has tasted the wonderful world God made for them, it is foolish. God said it.

Psalm 49:10 For he sees wise men die; Likewise the fool and the senseless person perish, And leave their wealth to others.

Psalm 92:6 A senseless man does not know, Nor does a fool understand this.

Psalm 94:8 Understand, you senseless among the people; And *you* fools, when will you be wise?

Psalm 107:17 Fools, because of their transgression, And because of their iniquities, were afflicted.

Proverbs 1:7 The fear of the Lord *is* the beginning of knowledge, *But* fools despise wisdom and instruction.

Proverbs 1:7 The fear of the Lord *is* the beginning of knowledge, *But* fools despise wisdom and instruction.

Proverbs 10:21 The lips of the righteous feed many, But fools die for lack of wisdom.

Proverbs 12:15 The way of a fool *is* right in his own eyes, But he who heeds counsel *is* wise.

Proverbs 13:20 He who walks with wise *men* will be wise, But the companion of fools will be destroyed.

Proverbs 14:7 Go from the presence of a foolish man, When you do not perceive *in him* the lips of knowledge.

Proverbs 15:5 A fool despises his father's instruction, But he who receives correction is prudent.

Proverbs 15:14 The heart of him who has understanding seeks knowledge, But the mouth of fools feeds on foolishness.

Proverbs 26:11 As a dog returns to his own vomit, *So* a fool repeats his folly.

Proverbs 30:32 If you have been foolish in exalting yourself, Or if you have devised evil, *put your* hand on *your* mouth.

Matthew 7:26 "But everyone who hears these sayings of Mine, and does not do them, will be like a foolish man who built his house on the sand:

1 Corinthians 1:18 For the message of the cross is foolishness to those who are perishing, but to us who are being saved it is the power of God.

1 Corinthians 1:23 but we preach Christ crucified, to the Jews a stumbling block and to the Greeks foolishness.

Galatians 3:3 Are you so foolish? Having begun in the Spirit, are you now being made perfect by the flesh?

Titus 3:9 But avoid foolish disputes, genealogies, contentions, and strivings about the law; for they are unprofitable and useless.

THINGS TO CHEW ON

We will be preceded by those that have died before us. Then we will go up to meet Jesus in the air.(Jesus said to praY that you may escape the tribulation to come…so pray!) So who are these people? Are they the ones that died before Jesus paid for sins? Are they the bodies of the spirits that have gone up before us? Are the spirits of our loved ones waiting in a holding place or did their spirits go right to heaven? What does the Bible say about it?

I Thess 4:16 For the Lord himself will descent from heaven with a cry of command, with the voice of an archangel, and with the sound of the trumpet of God. And the dead in Christ will rise first.

Daniel 12:2 Many of those who sleep in the dust of the earth shall awake, some to everlasting life and some to shame and everlasting contempt.

I Cor 15:52   In a moment, in the twinkling of an eye, at the last trumpet. For the trumpet will sound, and the dead will be raised imperishable and we shall be changed.

Matthew 27:52 The tombs also were opened. And many bodies of the saints who had fallen asleep were raised.

Isaiah 26:19 Your dead shall live; their bodies shall rise. You who dwell in the dust, awake and sing for joy! For your dew is a dew of light, and the earth will give birth to the dead.

I Thess. 4:15 For this we declare to you by a word from the Lord, that we who are alive, who are left until the coming of the Lord, will not precede those who have fallen asleep.

Acts 24:15 Having a hope in God, which these men themselves accept, that there will be a resurrection of both the just and the unjust.

John 14:3 And if I go and prepare a place for you, I will come again and will take you to myself, that where I am you may be also.

John 5:29… and come out, those who have done good to the resurrection of life, and those who have done evil to the resurrection of judgment.

Jude 1:6 And the angels who did not stay within their own position of authority, but left their proper dwelling, he has kept in eternal chains under gloom darkness until the judgment of the great day…

I Thess 4:17 Then we who are alive, who are left, will be caught up together with them in the clouds to meet the Lord in the air, and so we will always be with the Lord.

2 Cor. 5:8 Yes, we are of good courage, and we would rather be away from the body and at home with the Lord.

Daniel 12:1 At that time shall arise Michael, the great prince who has charge of your people and there shall be a time of trouble, such as never has been since there was a nation till that time. But at that time your people shall be delivered, everyone whose name shall be found written in the book.

Rev. 20:6 Blessed and holy is the one who shares in the first resurrection! Over such the second death has no power, but they will be priests of God and of Christ, and they will reign with him for a thousand years.

Rev. 20:1-15…saw the souls of those who had been beheaded for the testimony of Jesus…had not worshiped the beast or its image and had not received its mark on their foreheads or their hands. They came to life and reigned with Christ for a thousand years. The rest of the dead did not come to life until the thousand years were ended. This is the first resurrection.

John 5:28 Do not marvel at this, for an hour is coming when all who are in the tombs will hear his voice.

John 3:13 No one has ascended into heaven except he who descended from heaven, the Son of Man.

Matt 27:52-53 The tombs also were opened. And many bodies of the saints who had fallen asleep were raised, and coming out of the tombs after his resurrection they went into the holy city and appeared to many.

THE SALESMAN

You just got out of bed and there is a knock on the front door. Throw on clothes and run to answer it. There he stands, handsome guy, with a big smile on his cute face.

You open the door and he begins his spiel. He is really good at it. You are nearly drooling to buy anything he is selling by the time you hear it all. You invited him in, and before you know it, you have signed your name and bought what he wanted you to buy; whether you needed it, whether you wanted it, or could afford it. This guy was really good at it.

What if the man was someone else in disguise? What if Satan works this way? He comes to you as an angel of light. He knocks on the door. You leave the screen locked and listen. He is offering you something, and it appears you cannot refuse it. This item is free.

This is an allegory of the doctor sitting you down and offering you cancer. "I am sorry to bring bad tidings, but the results of all the tests reveal you have prostate cancer."

Do you buy into it? God tells us not to put our trust in man. He may even be telling you facts, but what is the difference between facts and truth-especially God's Truth?

How should we answer such a statement? Think a minute. God tells us in His Word that He is our Great Physician and heals all our diseases. He said nothing shall harm you. He says no plague will come near you. He says your faith will protect you. Believe Him. Reject the diagnosis. Don't open the screen door and let him come in.

Does this sound crazy to you? This is what the woman did who gave all her money to the doctors. "If I can just touch His hem, I will be made whole." It worked!

THE NO WORRY ZONE

Phil. 4:6-7 Be anxious for nothing. In prayer with supplication and thanksgiving make your requests to God.

Meditate on these things. Dissect them. Study the origins and meanings of words.

Phil. 4:8 Whatever is true, honest, just, pure, lovely, and of good report. If there is any virtue, if there is any praise, think on these things.

Humble yourself in the sight of the Lord.

I Cor 10:13 "No temptation has overtaken you except what is common to mankind. And God is faithful; he will not let you be tempted beyond what you can bear. He will provide a way out so you can endure it.

We can't stand alone. We need each other. A hand cut off dies. We need the body of Christ. The gifts are for the use of the body.

Did a door open that needed to be closed? If we sow to the flesh we reap destruction. Gal.6:8 If we sow to the spirit, we will reap eternal life.

What is the purpose of a law? For your protection.

No boundaries= no safety.

How do we know the Truth? We read. We have mentors. We pair up. (One turns away a thousand enemies. Two can turn away 10,000 in prayer.)

We take our thoughts captive.

2 Cor 10:3 We war in the spirit, not the flesh. Our weapons are mighty, to the pulling down of strongholds.

We cast down vain imaginations and take our thoughts captive. HALT=hungry/angry/lonely/tired.

Humble yourself or you will be humiliated. Not "I deserve." None deserve. It is all by grace.

Gluttony is also sin, looking for food for comfort, same as an alcoholic looks for relief in a counterfeit way. No difference.

Was Jesus tempted all ways? Yes!

What Job feared the most came upon him. Fear is your enemy. Fear involves health, wealth, loved ones and life itself.

Paul preached in Lystra and was stoned to death! He was dragged away and believers prayed. He came back! So fear nothing-even that!

THE SECRET OF POWER WITH GOD AND OF ALL DIVINE MIRACLES

Matthew 1:21 (NKJV) And she will bring forth a Son, and you shall call His name [a]JESUS, for He will save His people from their sins."

Mark 16:17-18 (NKJV)
[17] And these signs will follow those who [a]believe: In My name they will cast out demons; they will speak with new tongues; [18] they[b] will take up serpents; and if they drink anything deadly, it will by no means hurt them; they will lay hands on the sick, and they will recover."

John 1:[12] But as many as received Him, to them He gave the [a]right to become children of God, to those who believe in His name:

John 14:12 "Most assuredly, I say to you, he who believes in Me, the works that I do he will do also; and greater *works* than these he will do, because I go to My Father. [13] And whatever you ask in My name, that I will do, that the Father may be glorified in the Son. [14] If you [a]ask anything in My name, I will do *it.* [15]"If you love Me, [b]keep My commandments.

John 15:16 (NKJV) You did not choose Me, but I chose you and appointed you that you should go and bear fruit, and *that* your fruit should remain, that whatever you ask the Father in My name He may give you.

John 16:23-26 (NKJV) "And in that day you will ask Me nothing. Most assuredly, I say to you, whatever you ask the Father in My name He will give you. [24]Until now you have asked nothing in My name. Ask, and you will receive, that your joy may be full.

THE MAN WITH NO NAME

. We don't even know who he is. All we know is he got caught stealing, and paid with his life! What did he steal that was so valuable? Have you ever stolen anything? What a heavy penalty!

Not only that; he was tortured as well. But it was nothing like the man next to him! That one was scourged until he did not look human! A ring of long thorns was pressed into his skull! And finally his hands and feet were not tied but nailed to a tree with a crossbar.

The thief watched all this and joined the crowds mocking Jesus and challenging Him to save Himself.

None recalled He had told them the Son of Man would die and rise again. Mark 8:312 says it. Verse 34 says to take up our cross and follow Him.

But this thief was watching Jesus as He refused to be drugged, and asking God to forgive them! The thief hanging next to Jesus was beginning to realize this was no ordinary man!

Just before Jesus died, just in time, the thief said, "Lord, remember me when you come into your kingdom." (Had he been baptized? Still went with Jesus!)

Jesus shocked him with, "Today you will be with Me in paradise." Wow! Can you imagine his excitement? He went from terror to unspeakable joy! From hopelessness to faith! From being a sinner, turned into a new creature!

We will meet him someday.

www.bigstock.com · 22591739

THE LIGHT OVERCOMES THE DARKNESS

A revelation came to me tonight as I was preparing for bed that was exactly like a lightbulb coming on in a blackened room! Suddenly I realized the reason all my joints are tight, my back is in knots, and I can't totally relax and simply rest. This may explain why my blood pressure gradually began climbing to dangerous levels. I understand now why I lie awake at night until one or two, and then have trouble getting up in the morning. I know now why I snap at my husband at any minor statement that hints at criticism. I constantly try to busy myself at any task I can conjure up just to be doing something useful.

I became aware that behind my every motion, my every motive, and my every thought is the feeling of total worthlessness! Now that should not have been such a shock, except I had no clue that such feelings existed inside of me. I am amazed that it could have eluded me so long, but more amazed that it popped into my brain so quickly with such clarity! I suspect God had something to do with it. He has been known to do such things now and then.

When I cook, I am thinking in the back of my head that I should cook fancier meals, be more organized, be more original, have it ready sooner, or some other criticism dominates me while I am working. I have thought this way for years, but until tonight, I didn't pay attention to it.

When I work at being a good Grandma, I constantly berate myself for not being wiser, funnier, prettier, dress better, be more generous, or better in some way. When I clean, I am always thinking something is wrong with the way I am doing things. It is never right! It is never sufficient! No wonder when my husband says anything negative, I jump all over him and overreact. It is the straw that breaks a camel's back!

I have been trying to learn drawing and writing. The same condemning thoughts dominate absolutely everything I attempt to do. But it is covered up by smiles, jokes, small talk, and even I am unaware that "it" is speaking all the time, in undertones I had not 'heard' until now.

Now I hear them loud and clear. Since they have had light shed on them, these thoughts of mine, I recognize that it has not been my own voice or conscience at all! I am familiar with this liar who visits me, but didn't notice he had returned.

Thank you, Lord, for uncovering the deceiver, the accuser of the brethren, and shedding light on his destructive ways so I can see him. From now on, I can fight him off and restore my mind to sanity. This has gone on long enough. The Word of God will destroy him, and he will flee from me. I will resist the devil, submit to God, pick up my sword and my shield and all the other ammunition God has given me, and God will restore my sound mind, filled with love and power. Peace is again ruling in my heart, and it is wonderful! The blood of Jesus has set me free from condemnation!

"There is therefore now no condemnation to them which are in Christ Jesus, who walk not after the flesh, but after the Spirit." Romans 8:1

THE LAST DAYS AND WHAT TO WATCH OUT FOR

The key perversions of the **Cults** always relate to the central issues of theology, specifically the Doctrine of God, **Jesus** Christ, and Salvation. They are considered **Cults** because they seek to "counterfeit" Biblical Christianity. Counterfeits deceive by their outward appearance.

The Jesus of the Cults and religions

Another Jesus Today's new spirituality does include Jesus, but he is not the Jesus of Scripture. He is another Jesus who is appreciated by mystics and Gnostics alike. He is accepted by the other religions as a great teacher, an enlightened spiritual master, but not the Son of God, God in the flesh, the only Savior from our sins, and **<u>only way to the Father</u>**. He needs to be something other than the Bible's Jesus to be accepted by the masses.

SUPERMAN, AN ALLEGORY OF JESUS?

In 2006 I went to the movies and saw "Superman." It had violence, action, things exploding, machine guns, helicopters, people screaming and New York City getting demolished.

Superman returns from his destroyed planet after disappearing five years. Lois Lane gives up on him and has a son out of wedlock with Richard. Lex Luther suspects the child of being the son of Superman when he dumps a piano on a bad guy and kills him. But I see no evidence it was his.

Superman is sort of like a god. Some may see it as an allegory of Christ. He comes from another planet. He has a father who sends him to earth. He has no limitations. He is tortured by an evil power. He is said to have died. He returns to life. He destroys the works of the enemy. He has many followers. He is not recognized by those closest to him. He saves the world.

In the movie, Lex gets some Kryptonite and also goes to the planet and gets some crystals that can destroy New York City, turn out all power and create huge crystals in the ocean Lex calls "land."

The crystals lift up a ship as they grow from the sea. The shop cracks in half, locking three people in a hold full of water.

Superman sets them free. He fixes NYC, catches a ball in the sky, stops fires, robbers, plane crash, missile, and throws Lex's 'land' into space – phenomenal completely unbelievable stuff.

He is in love with Lois, but releases her, knowing he has a higher purpose.

So what do you think? Jesus could do all those things and more, but chooses to heal people instead.

THE BOOK OF ACTS

Luke is the author. It defines the spread of Christianity, the ministry of Paul to Gentiles, and the expansion of Mark 16:20. It describes the descent of Holy Spirit to the masses for the first time, enduing humans with power to do even more than Jesus did! It speaks of the Millenium: 1:6; 2:17-20; 3:19-21; 8:12; 14:22; 20:25 28:23,31. It reveals the controversy between Jews and Christians over the law. It is the model of the Christian church and the means of spreading the truth.

It begins with the last words of Jesus while He was on earth. He makes a promise that He will send down the Holy Spirit in just a few days. He had risen from being dead forty days before, and many witnesses can attest to that. It is the most profound event the world has ever seen.

His followers watch Him taken up in a cloud to heaven. They can't stop staring at the sky! It is unbelievable! They never saw a man fly! Finally a couple of angels show up and tell them He will be back someday the same way He left. Nobody had a clue it would not happen for a couple thousand years.

So everyone who heard His promise goes to Jerusalem to a room upstairs where some were staying. They pray and sing and fellowship with each other, but the crowd dwindles to 120, as nothing seems to happen. Finally, on the Day of Pentecost, guests from all over are in Jerusalem for the celebration.

This feast day began in Leviticus 23. God commanded His people on harvest day to take a sheaf of the first fruits of harvest to the priest, and wave it before God, along with a lamb as a burnt offering. They also mix fine flour with oil and offer it to God with a glass of wine. It sounds like a nice meal to me, meat, fruit, veggies, fresh bread and wine.

Count fifty days to the day after the seventh Sabbath and offer a new grain offering. Offer seven lambs, one bull and two rams, and burn them. Then sacrifice a kid and two male lambs as a peace offering.

All this is a symbol of the final offering of Jesus. He died on Good Friday and rose on Easter. Then he walked on earth forty days and left. How many days are there in seven Sabbaths? Forty-nine. And one more is fifty, or pente. So Jesus left earth nine days before Pentecost.

On the tenth day- Pentecost- the Holy Ghost poured into that room like a mighty wind! Tongues of fire sat on each head and they each began speaking in another language! They poured out of the building and still babbling, attracted the attention of all the foreigners. "They are speaking our languages! They are proclaiming the mighty works of God!" The news of Jesus death and resurrection gradually spread everywhere. So did the world change?

Oh, yes! The "religious legalists" began fighting against God's wonderful plan and power! Believers were persecuted, beaten and put in stocks in prisons. Jesus had warned this would happen. The devil began to get scared when he realized his demons were being cast out of possessed people. His kingdom had lost a lot of power, and God had empowered His people to conquer the devil. Jesus was gone, but His power remained. Do you see any parallels today?

Many Old Testament prophecies have been fulfilled in Acts. They are a separate lesson. They prove clearly that Jesus rose in the flesh and was not just a spirit, and a substitute did not take His place on the cross, as many believe.

The apostles and all the 120 began telling everyone about Jesus and salvation. "Repent and be baptized in Jesus' name and you shall receive the gift of the Holy Spirit." Thousands accepted Jesus as a result, and signs and wonders astonished them all. The believers even sold some of their possessions and with big generous hearts, shared with those in need. They met daily at the temple.

A man lame from birth got healed. Five thousand more got saved before long. The disciples preached and the place shook again and they were all filled with the Holy Spirit. Great grace was upon them all. None lacked. All shared. (Is this like ideal communism?)

Then Ananias and Sapphira lied about what they had given to the church and God struck them dead! Think that might happen today?

Before long, Peter was thrown into prison by dissenters and the high priest. But an angel opened the prison doors and brought out Peter and the other apostles. "Go stand in the temple and preach all the words of this life."

Stephen did great wonders and signs until he was criticized by the authorities and they stoned him to death!

How does this all parallel with Jesus' death, resurrection and the outpouring of His spirit? The timing lines up. Jesus was the wine offering and He was the bread offering. He said the bread is His body and the wine is His blood.

Then on day fifty, He sent His spirit. The fire could signify the altar fires that burned up the sacrifice. But why the tongues? What parallels that gift? When did God cause people to speak different languages and why? This is the only gift that had never occurred before.

Long ago Nimrod built a tower to reach heaven. God confused the language of the whole world! Nobody could communicate so they stopped building. Maybe it was a worship thing. Everyone dispersed and ended up populating the earth instead of congregating in one spot.

This language God gives when Jesus baptizes us is a sign His power has entered us. It is also power to pray in languages the devil cannot understand-called a mystery in the spirit. This is a plural gift. When you pray this way for a while, the language changes into a different one for some reason. Why? Some say it becomes intercession. I can't prove it but it is possible.

Is this gift the same one that manifests in church when one speaks in a tongue and another person is given the ability to interpret it for understanding? It does not appear to be. It is an additional gift for the whole body of Christ.

Those baptized with the Spirit shared everything they had with each other. None had lack. All had their needs met. Do we do that today? Should we?

Simon the sorcerer believed and got baptized. When he saw the Holy Spirit given to people, he offered money to have the same power to put his hands on people to get the Holy Spirit. Peter rebuked him for thinking it could be bought with money. It is free!

Holy Spirit told Philip to chase down a leader in Ethiopia in charge of the queen's treasury. He was riding a chariot through the desert toward home. Philip answered his questions and he got saved! Philip found water and baptized him. Then Philip got transported to a city fifty miles away! He just disappeared!

A man named Saul persecuted the believers and had them imprisoned and stood by when Stephen was stoned to death, agreeing with it. One day a light shone around him and he fell off his horse to the ground. Jesus spoke to him asking why he was persecuting Him. God struck him blind. He got his attention and ordered him to go to the city. Ananias obeyed God and found him. He put hands on him to receive his sight. So Saul became Paul, an apostle of Jesus. (Saul means "asked for, prayed for." Paul means small or humble!)

Peter healed a paralyzed man. Then Peter prayed and a dead woman named Dorcas came back to life! Many got saved over that miracle.

Cornelius, a Gentile centurion feared God, who gave him a vision of an angel. He said to send for Peter and told him the details, so he sent men to get Peter. In the meantime Peter went into a trance. He saw heaven open and a sheet opened up with animals in it. God said, "Kill and eat." He argued. "Old T. law said not to eat those things!"

"What God has cleansed you must not call common."

HS told him three men were seeking him. "Go with them." So Peter got a chance to tell Cornelius about Jesus, His resurrection, the baptism and the HS.

At one point a prophet, Agabus said there was coming a great famine throughout the entire world! It occurred in the days of Claudius Caesar. I wonder why? God told the prophet; to warn them to save up food?

Then Herod killed John's brother James with a sword! He put Peter in prison with many guards. The night before Herod was going to bring him out to deal with him, Peter was asleep, in chains. An angel struck him. The chains fell off. He thought he was dreaming but followed him out and the angel disappeared.

Our grandson Mitch as a little boy woke from a dream after his baby sister died at age one month. Robin was beautiful and had wings! She told Mitch who she was and said that Jesus is coming soon, when men control life with science. What does that mean? We found out how to abort babies, give morphine to dying people to speed it up, and do amazing surgeries to save lives. We use science instead of depending on God to supernaturally heal us. One morning when Mitch was only four or five, he said, "Jesus is coming back when man creates life." He had no idea God was speaking through him! Wht does that mean?

God showed me another thing. God told Abraham to sacrifice his son Isaac, his ONLY son! So did God not consider Ishmael Abe's son?

PRAISE AND THE POWER
IN OUR TONGUE

We enter His gates with thanksgiving and into His courts with praise. Enter the Holy of Holies with worship. Worship means to feel or express reverence or adoration to God.

Life and death is in the power of our tongue. God tells us to choose life and blessing and not death or cursing and we will live.

We are not entitled to anything as humans, but we are offered many things as children of God through Jesus and His blood. In our flesh there is no good thing.

What is in your heart? It will come out of your mouth.

Curses are a result of ingratitude. Dt. 28:45 Num. 31:48

Tithes are a result of being grateful for God and His blessings. Luke 7:36

God said I will meet all your needs through Christ and His riches in glory.

Call things that are not as though they were and they shall be.

When the enemy comes in like a flood God will raise up a standard against him.

Ask anything in My name, Jesus said, and your Father in heaven will give it to you, if it lines up with His will.

Call on the elders when you are sick and they will anoint you with oil. The prayer of faith will heal you.

No weapon formed against you will prosper.

No harm shall come near your dwelling.

A double minded man receives nothing from God.

Transform your mind into the mind of Christ.

By His stripes you are healed.

More study: confirmations:
Exodus 15:26, 23:25-26
Dt. 7:14-16; Dt. 30:19-20
I Kings 8:50
Ps. 103:1-5; Ps. 91:9-10;14-16; Ps. 118:17
Prov 4:20-24
Isaiah 41:10
Is. 53:4-5
Jer 1:12; 17:14; 30:17
Joel 3:10
Nahum 1:9
Matt. 21:21-22
Mark 9:23-24; 10:2; 11:22-24; 16:14-18
Luke 6:19; 9:2; 13:16
Acts. 5:16; 10:38
Romans 4:16-21; 8:2,11
2 Corinthians 4:18; 10:3-5
Galatians 3:13-14,29
Ephesians 6:10-17
Phil. 2:13; 4:6-9
2 Timothy 1:7

Hebrews 10:23,35-36; 11:11; 13:18
James 4:7; 5:14-16
I Peter 2:24
I John 3:21-22; 5:14-15
3 John 2
Revelation 12:11

GOD'S LAWS FOR HEALING

Cooperate with God. Mark 6:5 Jesus could not heal those in His own home town. Familiarity breeds contempt? Resist the devil. God cannot lie. Matt 13:57 Unbelief blocks healing. I Tim 3:16 Jesus is God. I Peter 2:24 Matt 10:1 We have authority. Matt. 10:8 Go. Heal the sick.

You already have it. 2 Peter 3:9 God wants us well. Eph 3:20 He can do anything. His power works in us. Man's ignorance kept us from using electricity, though it was always there- for thousands of years!

We do not get well by begging. Rom 3:27 Law of faith. The power is at my command. God is the source of the power. The power was put in us. We must learn how to utilize it. How do we release it?

3 John 1:2 Do not say "if it is Your will." This reveals ignorance of His will and reveals our doubt. A double minded man gets nothing from God! His will is very clear. My people perish for lack of knowledge.

Jesus sent His word and healed them. By our words we are justified or condemned. Life and death is in the power of the tongue.

MONOGAMOUS MARRIAGE IS BEST

Jacob was not monogamous. I am not sure how many wives he had but ten of his sons were from different wives, Leah, Bilhah and Zilpah. Joseph was born to Jacob's real love, Rachel. Benjamin was born to her later when she died of childbirth.

Joseph's mom and dad must have given him enough love to be self-assured, but his brothers all hated him. Reuben and Judah were the only two that were against killing him, though, when they had the chance. Maybe they had a kind mother.

When Joseph shared his dreams with the brothers, they were enraged. "We are going to bow down to you?" The seed was planted. "We are getting rid of this one." That means they believed his dream, doesn't it?

Jacob sent Joseph to the fields to find his brothers and bring word that they were all right. They saw the chance to kill him, but Reuben talked them into putting him in an empty cistern, planning to rescue him later. While Reuben was out of sight, Judah convinced the brothers to sell him to some foreign Ishmaelites as a slave. (Ishmael was Abraham's child with Sarah's slave.) Reuben was distraught when he found him gone. I wonder if they ever told him what they did.

So God's plan was enacted. The dream would one day come to pass. I find it interesting that God in the OT would kill people for being evil, but not in the NT. Judah got married, had a son who married Tamar. But the son was evil so God killed him! Judah gave Tamar to the next son, and he was evil, too, by refusing to impregnate Tamar, so God killed him too!

Tamar was ordered to wait for another son to grow up and give her a baby, but when he was ready, Judah refused to give him to her. He feared losing yet another son! So she decided to get a baby another way. Why did she not just leave and find herself a husband? Instead she dressed up as a prostitute and Judah came along. He did not recognize her and took her to bed. So the men could do what they wanted for sex, but the women would be killed if they were loose?

She took his staff, seal and cord as a pledge of later payment. He got her pregnant. Her father-in-law was going to have her burned to death! She brought out his staff and proved he was the father! Whew! That staff saved her life! Tamar had twins, Zerah (brightness) and Perez (means breaking out.)

As we know, the dreams came true years later. The brothers came to Egypt where Joseph ruled under the Pharaoh and was in charge of the food storage for the country during a famine. They came to get food, and ended up bowing to Joseph.

Eventually Joseph revealed his identity, forgave the brothers and saved all their lives. Pharaoh gave permission for them to come live in his country.

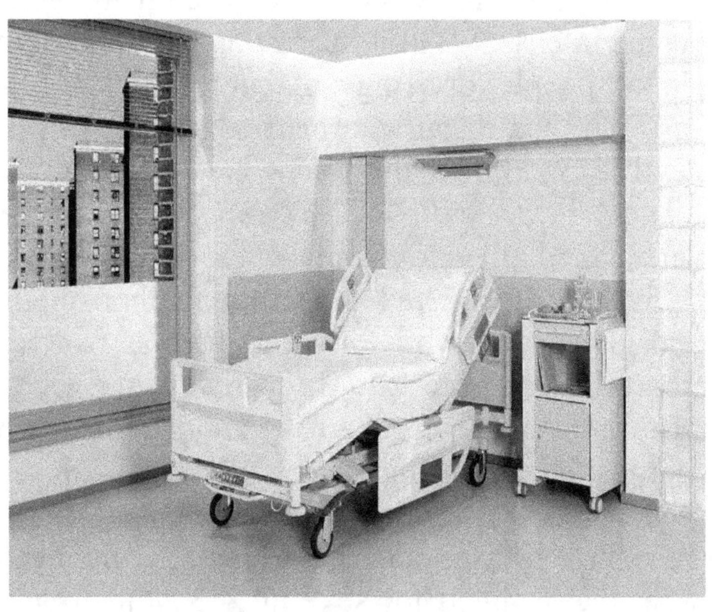

My Testimony

I will close with my story that began April 9 of 2020.

Carrying my sweet puppy up a hill, I suddenly lost my breath! I collapsed on the ground panting! Corona virus! Oh no! Within an hour I was in Emergency being tested. But I was negative. So what was it? They took a sample of blood and stuck me right in the hospital! They found I had lost half my blood!

I was diagnosed with a leaking mitral valve, bleeding ulcers (from a prescription), a 90% blocked major heart artery, and obviously had just had a mild heart attack! I was suddenly scheduled for open heart surgery! I never felt a thing. For being eighty, I am still able to do everything I could do at fifty!

I had never been confronted with such things! I never had to stand on the Word for them. I was rarely at all sick. God said, "You may let the doctor operate or you can let the Great Physician heal you supernaturally. Which do you prefer?"

Well, you know that answer! I got so excited I could hardly speak when the doctor came in. "I have decided to go home and reconsider my options." He said," Oh, we do have other options!" Hmm. Surprise. Well, I didn't choose those either. I asked about his beliefs and he has not yet decided whether God exists or not! (I'm gone!)

He wouldn't let me leave without a stress test, which I passed with flying colors! MRI before and after-all was well. Praise God!

So I am doing what God's Word tells me to do. He said once I choose to trust Him, I must not be double minded or I am in trouble. He said to stand firm in faith and confess with my mouth what I truly believe in my heart. I believe God. I know His voice and knew it was Him. I am not saying anyone else should do this, but it was my experience alone. If the doctor diagnoses you, you need not argue. It is his statement of symptoms leading him to a conclusion. You will come to a conclusion based on what Jesus says to you and did for you.

The Holy Spirit clearly spoke, first to me, and then confirmed it to my son Dave, who didn't even know this was going on, and he texted me after I had made my decision.

Your Bible is your final authority, not human wisdom. We live in another realm with different methods. Seek the promises on healing. Become convinced God's will is healing for you, and it is already dealt with.

It was God's will that all be saved but they didn't. Not all get healed either for the same reason. Many are dead. It's none of my business why. Most did not believe it. Respond to the Word! Luke 5:12-13 says if you will…of course I will….be healed. And the man's leprosy disappeared!

I'm glad the doctor found it. Now I can deal with it and put it to bed forever. This test of faith will benefit me the rest of my life for other situations and other people as well. I needed to learn God does not lie and that a leap of faith is just that. I may not always be able to take that leap, but God gave me a special understanding I did not have before.

I have no fear of catching the Covid virus going around. My son and his invalid wife came down with it while I was spending time with them, I continued to care for them and did not catch it. The Word worked for me. I am not saying others should do that. My experience just helped me not to fear it.

I Peter 2:24 Jesus bore our sins and our sicknesses. I am healed by His stripes. He paid long ago for this very moment. It is finished.

Now we need to overcome stress, fear, worry, and unbelief. Serving others, laughing-good medicine, and praising God helps a lot! We 'labor to rest.'

I John 4:19 Believe God loves you! Take communion. It reminds you of what Jesus did, even if you use o.j. and a cookie. Treat it as a medicine. John 6:48-58.

I Cor. 10:5. Take authority over negative thoughts. Satan's weapon is suggestion. He can only feed your mind. Your own mind grabs it and does the damage. He was stripped of his authority to do any more. It may even be that he brings sickness only by suggestion and our body may do the rest- my opinion. Cast down imaginations that bring you harm. Fill your heart with the word of God. Don't test yourself to see if you really believe. And be ready when Satan tries to give you symptoms again. Use your authority to command him to leave, and plead the blood of Jesus, which is why we have authority!

Understand spiritual warfare and how it works. What did Jesus say to the devil in the desert when he left Him alone? "It is written…" Find sword verses to knock him in the head!

Ephesians 6:10 says it is a done deal. The devil uses symptoms and thoughts and bad reports to scare you and veer you off that narrow path.

I Thess 5:6-18 speaks about praise breaking the yoke of bondage! Satan hates it! He sticks his fingers in his ears and runs away screaming!

After a month of feeling great after leaving the hospital, I got attacked! I couldn't catch my breath! The doctor had said to watch out for that-first sign of trouble. It started at 5 AM when my puppy started barking for no reason. Maybe he saw that demon in my room, eh?

First fear hit me and I was tempted to go to Emergency. But God's words came to me. I started meditating on those powerful promises. I was not healed because of how I felt but because it was offered and paid for. I could let it go and have surgery if need be…or stand firm, not waver in faith and not be double minded. God had already warned me it would hit, so it wasn't a big shock.

All the way to church I sang with praise music. When I arrived, I told a friend and we prayed. I confessed my healing and my belief, and within minutes my breathing became steady and slow! Joy filled my heart! I will be passing a test from the doctor one of these days, but no matter what it shows, I will stand on God's promises!

A friend shared after church that she had a mass in her stomach for several weeks. The doctor found it. She simply spoke God's promises on healing every day. It grew bigger and bigger over the months! She kept speaking health to her body in Jesus' name. One morning she woke up and it was completely gone!! God is not a liar! And He loves us!

I have been examined recently and was given a clean bill of health. I am so happy!

The author teaches Sunday School in Norcross, Georgia and is a compulsive writer! During the Covid crisis, she got bored. This is the result. I hope some of it answers questions you may have had, and she hopes it cleared it up. There are likely no two Christians who agree on everything. As long as we all know Jesus, thank Him for dying in our place and taking our punishment, and we know He rose from the dead, the rest will get settled in heaven- in a New York Minute!

Judy has published about twenty-six books you can find at Amazon.com. They are all true stories and testimonies. Some are under her pen name, Victoria Vos.

She was born in Holland, Michigan in 1940 and moved to Georgia in 1976 with her husband who worked at Herman Miller Furniture. They have three sons, David, Tom and Rob, eight grandkids, 13 or more great grands and now two great-great grandchildren. Roger passed away in 2010, so Judy has decided to write as a way to share her vision for the future.

LUISA GOMEZCOELLO

GOTITAS DE COSMOS

Luisa Gomezcoello es una poeta ecuatoriana, nacida en Azogues. Terminó sus estudios de medicina en Quito y Medellín. Durante su larga carrera de médica, siempre mantuvo un interés apasionado por el mundo literario, y por fin tenemos el honor de publicar la primera parte de sus obras.

Sus tres hijos José, Ronny y Natalia saben desde pequeños de su gusto por el multicolor de las flores y por la inconmensurabilidad de las estrellas; y de su cariño sin fin por la igualdad y por el amor a la dignidad y esperanza de todo ser viviente.

Fuerte en sus convicciones y al mismo tiempo decidida y dulce en su mirada, ella nos cobija hoy con la tibia belleza cristalina de sus poemas.